Cornerstones of Freedom

The Story of
THE HOMESTEAD ACT

By R. Conrad Stein

Illustrated by Cathy Koenig

CHILDRENS PRESS, CHICAGO

Library of Congress Cataloging in Publication Data

Stein, R   Conrad.
  The story of the Homestead act.

  (Cornerstones of freedom)
  SUMMARY: Discusses the 1804 Homestead act that
offered United States citizens and immigrants large
tracts of inexpensive land on the Great Plains.
  1. Frontier and pioneer life—The West—Juvenile
literature. 2. Homestead law—The West—Juvenile
literature. 3. The West—History—1848-1950—Juvenile
literature. [1. Frontier and pioneer life—The West.
2. Homestead law—The West. 3. The West—History—
1848-1950] I. Koenig, Cathy. II. Title.
F596.S83   978′.02   78-4839
ISBN 0-516-04616-0

3 4 5 6 7 8 9 10 11 12 R 85 84 83 82

"Go West, young man," wrote Horace Greeley, editor of the New York *Tribune*. Before the Civil War, many Americans took Greeley's advice. They went at first to trap animals for fur and to trade with the Indians. Then gold was discovered in California, and thousands headed West to seek their fortunes. These early settlers raced to California.

Hardly anyone stopped in the Great Plains states of Iowa, Kansas, Nebraska, and the Dakotas. Why should they? There wasn't much there but an ocean of grass and roving herds of buffalo. The land baked under the relentless summer sun, and there were few trees to break the winds of the constant winter blizzards. Who would want to live in the Great Plains?

In spite of the hardships, however, thousands of men and women who dreamed of owning a farm did want to live there. They were a different breed from those fortune-seekers and adventure-hunters who had journeyed West in earlier years. The new settlers did not wish to strike it rich and then move on. They wanted instead to establish farms that they could work and then pass on to their children. These were the settlers who would finally tame the Wild West.

"Uncle Sam is rich enough to give us all a farm." These words from a popular song sung in the 1850s were true. The United States Government owned endless square miles of grassland west of the Missouri River. The government wanted to encourage settlement on this vast frontier, but had no definite policy as to how to distribute the land. It took Abraham Lincoln, himself a frontiersman, to establish a policy.

When Lincoln became President, he backed an astonishing proposal that became known as the Homestead Act. Under the act any man or woman could acquire a 160-acre farm "for the purpose of actual settlement and cultivation." Never again would a government give away so much land to the people. The applicant for a land grant did not even have to be a citizen of the United States. He merely had to declare his intention to become a citizen. Those applying would not be given final deed to the property for five years. Then they had to convince the government that they had been living on the land and working it. Usually a plowed field and a home were sufficient proof.

The land was not entirely free. A filing fee of eighteen dollars was charged for each grant. Eighteen dollars for 160 acres came to about eleven cents an acre—an amazing bargain.

City dwellers in the eastern United States now dreamed about going West to farm. Eastern farmers, dissatisfied with their land, began to look at maps of Kansas and Nebraska.

The Homestead Act had perhaps its greatest impact across the Atlantic Ocean in Europe. Endless generations of European peasants had never owned land of their own. They had tilled the farms of the upper classes since the time of feudalism. Could it be true, the peasants asked each other, that the government of the United States was really willing to give away such large farms even to people who were not citizens? When they found that it was indeed true, they flocked to the New World by the shipload.

President Lincoln signed the Homestead Act on May 20, 1862. The law provided that actual homesteading could start on January 1, 1863. For thousands it was an impossible dream come true. A farmer, no matter how poor, would finally be able to have a farm of his own.

At the time of the passage of the Homestead Act, however, the Civil War was raging in the United States. Every day hundreds of potential farmers were being slaughtered on battlefields.

The first applicant for land under the Homestead Act was Daniel Freeman, a soldier in the Union Army. He was on furlough when he applied for a land grant near the town of Beatrice, Nebraska, on December 31, 1862. Since he had to rejoin his regiment the next day, the other applicants let him go to the head of the line. Thus Daniel Freeman became the first "homesteader." There would be thousands more.

When the Civil War ended, homesteaders poured across the Missouri River to stake out farms in Kansas and Nebraska. Many were

single men and some were single women, but the majority were families. They soon learned that having free land did not free them from toil. The Great Plains was an endless prairie of waist-high buffalo grass whipped by a whistling wind. The soil was matted with thick roots. No plow had ever cut through this tough sod.

As the settlers traveled West they saw hundreds of prairie dog villages from their wagons. The chattering little animals had created whole communities by burrowing into the ground. Few homesteaders thought that they, too, would soon be living the way the prairie dogs did. On the treeless prairie the homesteader would have to build his house from the only material available to him—the sod under his feet. The Great Plains earned the nickname "the sod house frontier."

The easiest type of house to build was the dugout. The homesteader selected a hill that was perhaps six or seven feet high and dug it out un-

til it became a room with three walls. The front wall was made by picking out the thickest chunks of sod that had been overturned when the farmer plowed his field. These chunks were cut into rectangular bricks one or two feet long. They were stacked to form a wall in the same way clay house bricks would be stacked. The roof was made from whatever wood could be found, prairie grass, and, again, more sod. Each dugout had a stove with a chimney poking up through the roof. Because no wood was available, the settler burned the dried-out dung of buffalo and cattle.

Living in a dugout was like living in a cave. It was impossible to keep out worms, spiders, or flies, and it was always dark and cold. Economy was the only advantage to a dugout. One Nebraska homesteader added up the expenses of constructing his home:

one window	$1.25
18 feet of lumber for door	.54
latch and hanging	.50
stove pipe to go through roof	.30
3 lbs. nails to make door	.19
total	$2.78

As the months passed, grass grew over the dugout and the settler's house looked like the rest of the landscape. One young girl wrote about one of the hazards of living in a sod house: "I was awakened by the noise of a terrible crash and I heard the mooing of a cow. My mother struck a match to the candle, and in the middle of the room stood our cow, Tillie. She had been grazing on the roof when she broke through."

A second type of home was the one made entirely of dried sod bricks. Someone with a sense of humor called this material "prairie marble." Hundreds of these sod houses sprouted up in Kansas and Nebraska. Sod was also used to construct churches, schools, stores, and post offices.

Living under a sod roof was an ordeal that can scarcely be imagined today. It not only leaked during a rain, but continued to do so for days afterward because the sod had become saturated. One woman remembered frying the morning pancakes while her daughter held an umbrella above her and the stove. A popular song among the homesteaders began with these words:

> My house is constructed of natural soil,
> The walls are erected according to Hoyle,
> The roof has no pitch, but is level and plain,
> And I never get wet till it happens to rain.

Although the soil of the Great Plains was useful for building houses, growing crops in it was another matter. For thousands of years the prairie had been alternately baked by torrid summers and then frozen by near-Arctic winters. It could produce seas of grass that nourished the herds of buffalo that in turn fed the plains Indians. But could it produce crops?

Early attempts at farming were discouraging. Iron plows that had been in use for years bent out of shape when a farmer tried to plow the tough prairie soil. Centuries of buffalo grass had left the soil with an armor of thick roots. Before the Civil War, however, a blacksmith from Vermont named John Deere had fashioned a new plow. His plow, of sharp, hard steel, cut through the prairie sod and turned it over neatly.

The wheat that was to grow on the prairie came not from the United States, but from far-off Russia. It was at first thought that the hard prairie soil would not produce wheat, but a stubborn group of European immigrants refused to believe this. Years earlier, a group of Germans had moved to Russia seeking religious freedom. Not finding freedom under the czars, they came next to the United States. The Germans brought with them bushels of Turkey Red wheat. This strain of wheat thrived in Russia, where the sod was also hard and the winters were severe. Soon Turkey Red wheat was growing on the small homesteads of the Great Plains.

The invention of barbed wire was a great benefit to the homesteader. Wooden fences could not be built, and animals quickly learned to push through fences of plain wire. Then someone observed that animals avoid thorny bushes. Why not attach thorns to plain wire? The idea was a success. Finally the homesteader could stop worrying about whether his neighbor's cow was trampling down his wheat. Soon the Great Plains were covered with a patchwork of farms, all neatly bordered with barbed wire.

These farms, however, encroached on another, older way of life. Years before the homesteaders had staked out their farms, a cattle empire had been established in Texas. Cattle were fattened on the Texas ranges, and then were driven north over the Great Plains to the railheads in Missouri. But by the 1870s the Great Plains region was no longer open prairie. Hundreds of farmers with patches of barbed wire fences blocked the way of the cattle drives.

A war broke out between the homesteaders and the cattle ranchers. This war would later become the subject of dozens of Western movies and hundreds of novels. At first it was a war of harassment. Ranchers warned new homesteaders about tribes of hostile Indians living in the

area. Actually, most of the plains Indians had disappeared with the buffalo, but some homesteaders were frightened away. The scare tactics worked particularly well with homesteaders from Europe who had read Wild West stories claiming that American Indians were cannibals. The war heated up when ranchers tore down barbed wire fences and drove their cattle over growing wheat fields. Homesteaders, in turn, fired shots at night to stampede large herds of cattle.

Harassment gave way to shooting when home-steads began to spring up on land the ranchers believed belonged to them. The conflict was relieved somewhat when the railroads extended into Texas, eliminating the need for long cattle drives. In the end, the war was won by the homesteaders, mainly because of their greater numbers.

Nature herself was a far more formidable enemy of the homesteader than were the cattle ranchers. The sun broiled the land during the summers, and the winters brought months of freezing temperatures and constant biting winds. Flooding was common in the spring, and lack of rain during the summer often stunted the growth of the crops. An unfortunate homestead-er could be flooded out and later grow a crop damaged by drought, all in the same year.

If Nature was an enemy, her most frightening single weapon was the simple grasshopper. These insects had always lived in the buffalo grass, but when that grass was replaced with wheat and corn, their population exploded.

The year 1874 had been a bountiful year for crops. Just before harvest time that year, the wheat and corn were tall and healthy. One Kansas family had just sat down to dinner. A boy stepped outside to the well for a pitcher of water. Above the horizon he saw a curious dot in the sky. As it moved closer, it took the form of a black storm cloud. The boy heard a high-pitched whirring noise.

"Grasshoppers!" he shouted. "Hoppers!"

The entire family left their dinners still steaming on the table and rushed outside. Grasshoppers covered them like snowflakes during a blizzard. Desperately, they grabbed brooms, shovels, and rakes and swung at the grasshoppers, trying to drive the insects out of their fields. Their fight was hopeless. In less than a half hour the grasshoppers had destroyed the work of a full year. They had devoured the family's entire wheat crop right down to the roots.

That year on the Great Plains was one long nightmare. A prevailing wind started in the Dakotas and swept down to northern Texas, taking with it enough hungry grasshoppers to darken the sun. Like a giant buzz saw the cloud of insects swarmed over the golden wheat fields, leaving behind them only black earth. The

prairie farmers, most of whom had studied the Bible, felt as if they were living through a plague such as those that had hit ancient Egypt. It was said that the grasshoppers were so thick that year that at one point they actually stopped a train on the Kansas Pacific Line.

Nature, sometimes brutal and sometimes beneficial, always treated the farmers equally. A disaster such as the grasshopper plague of 1874 struck not just one farmer, but all farmers for miles around. The one institution that gave comfort and hope to grieving farmers was their church. Together in church they would seek spiritual relief from the problems of the current year, and pray for better fortune the following year. Most of the homesteading families had been deeply religious before they went West. Those who had not been religious found themselves praying to God after one or two winters on the Great Plains.

Homesteading was too grueling a life for many. In one year alone, thirty thousand homesteaders abandoned their land and returned to the East. One east-bound wagon displayed a sign that read, "In God we trusted, in Kansas we busted." But for every homesteader who quit, a dozen more stayed, praying for a better year. Eventually they were rewarded.

As bleak as prairie life was, people were always able to find a means of enjoying themselves.

Homesteaders were great visitors. Farms were widely scattered in the early days of homesteading, and weeks could go by during which a homestead family saw no neighbors at all. Then, on a Sunday morning, a wagon containing a family of friends from a farm miles away would clang down the road. The children would play and the adults would talk. Since there were no telephones to announce them, these visits were always spontaneous.

The people of prairie towns took a lively interest in competitive sports. Horse races and foot races were popular. People gambled on local favorites. One story told of a young man who rode into a Kansas town and challenged anyone to a foot race. The fastest youth in the community was summoned. The outsider covered all bets. Just as the race was about to begin the stranger stripped off his outer clothing, revealing a track uniform underneath. The townspeople gasped. This young man was a professional. But the pride of the community was at stake, and no one withdrew his bet. The local boy became a hero that day by running the race of his life and beating the outsider by several feet. The stranger had to walk out of the town, as he had gambled his horse on the outcome of the race.

Knowledge of the game of baseball spread from the East to all parts of the nation during the Civil War. Many men who had learned the game brought it with them to the prairies. Because the homesteader could not buy a baseball at the local store, balls were made from the yarn of old woolen socks. The yarn was wound tightly into the size of a ball and then covered with leather from an old shoe. Bats were carved from the hardest wood that could be found. Freakish scores were recorded by teams playing in high grass and without the use of gloves. In August of 1871, a team from Milford, Nebraska played a team from neighboring Seward. The game lasted four hours and the final score was Milford 97, Seward 25.

The real heroes of prairie settlement were the women. They worked in the sod houses that could not be kept clean. They also did heavy work in the fields. They sewed by candlelight until late at night. They recorded births and deaths in the family Bible. Their stability would

give the frontier something it had never had—a recorded past.

The scenery was unchanging on the Great Plains, yet the prairie had its own kind of beauty. Perhaps only a woman's sensitivity could perceive it during those difficult times. It is not surprising that the best books to come out of the sod house frontier were written by women.

Willa Cather traveled with her family to a Nebraska farm in the 1880s, when she was only ten. She was fascinated one day by the sight of rolling waves of buffalo grass being moved gently by a whispering wind. She later wrote about this vision in her lovely book, *My Antonia*:

> As I looked about me I felt that the grass
> was the country, as the water is the sea.
> The red of the grass made all the great prairie
> the color of wine-stains, or of certain seaweeds
> when they are first washed up. And there
> was so much motion in it; the whole country
> seemed, somehow, to be running.

Gradually, technology made life on the Great Plains more livable.

Because there were so few hills and trees, an ever-present feature of prairie life was a constant wind. This wind was a ready source of power. Water lay deep below the surface on the plains. A farmer spent months drilling a well. Then he might spend an hour each day pumping the water up by hand. In the 1870s a small windmill was developed for home and farm use. Now the backbreaking job of pumping could be turned over to the steady prairie wind. Windmills became as common on the prairie as television antennas are on suburban homes today.

Machine farming started when a Virginian named Cyrus McCormick invented the reaper. Before the reaper, wheat was cut by hand with a scythe exactly as it had been harvested in Europe five hundred years earlier. Using McCormick's new machine, one man and a team of horses could do the work of five field hands. Later the reaper was improved so that it not only cut the wheat, but also tied it into neat bundles. Mechanical corn planters and cutters also appeared.

Production on homestead farms increased as much as five or six times when the new machines came into use. This increase came just in time, for while the frontier was developing, the population of the United States jumped from thirteen million to sixty million in only forty years. The Great Plains was the "breadbasket" feeding a growing country.

Farming in the prairie states contributed to the growth of a great American city. During the close of the last century, Chicago was the fastest growing city in the world. Wheat harvested in the prairies was shipped by rail to grain exchanges in Chicago. Machines to ease the toil of farmers were made in Chicago factories.

The greatest improvement in the lot of the prairie farmer came with the development of the railroads. During the late 1860s and the 1870s construction crews slammed down track in Kansas and Nebraska. Soon endless lines of track stretched across the Great Plains. Lumber, cheap and plentiful in the East, had been a luxury in the prairies. Now railroads delivered wood, and frame houses popped up to replace the cold, dark houses of sod.

If machine farming and railroads were a boon to the prairie farmer, these improvements also came with a price. A desire for independence was the major reason a farmer came West to settle. Initially he had independence, as his homestead provided the farmer with all he needed. He rarely had money, but little money was needed on the Great Plains.

Then came the railroads and the machines. The farmer discovered that if he specialized in just one crop, such as wheat or corn, he could sell his crop for cash at the end of the year. This put money in the farmer's pocket, but also made him dependent on the merchants in Chicago. And if he had one bad year, the farmer had to mortgage his land to the bank in order to borrow the cash he needed to operate the following year. He also had to pay interest on the loan. So the once independent farmer found himself dependent on banks, merchants, and the railroads that took his produce to market.

Still the homesteaders flooded to the free land. Iowa, Kansas, and Nebraska were quickly occupied. Thousands of homesteaders then turned north to the Dakotas. Others followed the railroads west to Colorado, Wyoming, Montana, and Washington.

Along with the legitimate homesteaders came the speculators. They wanted only to lay claim to free land and then wait a few years, hoping prices would go up so they could sell out for a profit. A great deal of fraud occurred, especially during the later period of homesteading.

The law said the land had to be cultivated before the homesteader could receive the final deed to his property. The speculator threw a few kernels of corn on the ground and called that cultivation. The government also wanted a house on the property as proof that it was being farmed. One man devised a house on wheels so that when a government inspector was in the area he could move the house to a speculator's property and charge the speculator daily rent.

As more and more homesteaders went West, free land became more and more scarce. Finally, there was only one remaining frontier. In the late 1880s the government acquired millions of acres when the Indians in the Oklahoma Territory were forced to give up their land. It was announced that the territory would be open to settlement at noon on April 22, 1889.

On the morning of April 22, a crowd estimated at one hundred thousand milled about the border of the new territory. There were men on horse-

back who hoped to race ahead of the crowd and claim the best land. Others waited in wagons, and some were on foot. The Santa Fe Railroad provided fifteen special trains, all jammed with eager settlers. A newspaper reporter noticed two or three men waiting to pedal into the territory on bicycles.

At noon a soldier on a hill sounded a bugle. Another dropped a signal flag, and the mad scramble began. Wagons, horses, trains, and bicycles all raced into the territory. Someone said it looked "like a human stampede." In less than twenty-four hours the land-hungry settlers had gobbled up two million acres of land. The last of the great land giveaways was over.

Though most of the homesteaders waited until the noon hour to start their dash, a few cheated and sneaked into the territory before twelve o'clock. Ironically, Oklahoma is named after those cheats—the Sooner State.

By 1890 the American census bureau claimed that "there can hardly be said to be a frontier line." Homesteaders had moved onto practically every area where the land could support a farm. The settlement of the frontier was over after just thirty years.

Homesteading started in the Great Plains states of Kansas, Nebraska, and Iowa. Now, in the overpopulated 1970s, wheat from those states has prevented starvation in some far-off corners of the world. The United States is one of the few countries that has harvests so abundant that it can afford to export millions of tons of food each year. The rich black soil of the Great Plains produces a large portion of this harvest. The homesteader breaking sod in the buffalo grass one hundred years ago could not have realized that his land would someday feed the world.

The sod house frontier looks different today. There are few patchwork farms separated by barbed wire fences. Farming is now big business. Today, fields of golden wheat and tall green corn stretch the length of the horizon as far as the eye can see. The wheat is harvested by giant self-propelled combines that in one day do the work of an army of early homesteaders.

On the lonely roads of Kansas or Nebraska some small farmers are still at work. Men and women sit on tractors that drag pieces of harvesting equipment. Most of the tractors are probably more than ten years old, and the engines sputter. The machines behind the tractors are almost museum pieces. The land these small farmers work was probably inherited from great-grandfathers who were homesteaders. It took a combination of faith, stubbornness, and hard work for those early homesteaders to build a farm and harvest crops. But the homesteaders believed that a farm is the best possible place to raise a family. The small farmers of today have inherited that same spirit.

About the Author

R. Conrad Stein was born and grew up in Chicago. He enlisted in the Marine Corps at the age of eighteen, and served for three years. He then attended the University of Illinois, where he received a Bachelor's Degree in history. He later studied in Mexico and earned a Master of Fine Arts degree from the University of Guanajuato. He now lives in Mexico, where he is a member of the PEN writers group of San Miguel de Allende.

The study of history is Mr. Stein's hobby. Since he finds it to be an exciting subject, he tries to bring the excitement of history to his readers. He is the author of many other books, articles, and short stories written for young people.

About the Artist

Cathy Koenig grew up in the northwest suburbs of Chicago, and moved into the city in 1966. She served an apprenticeship and later did some illustration during her four-year employment with a major Chicago art studio. Since that time, she has been free-lancing, working in advertising, children's book illustration, and greeting card illustration.